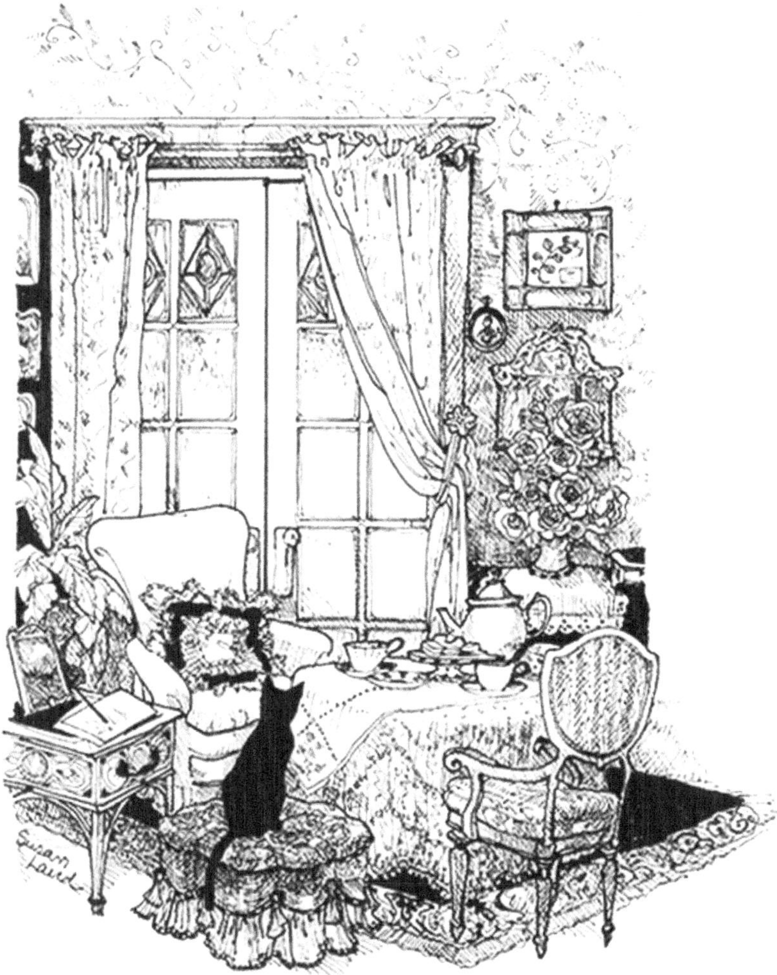
Susan Laird

Musings With a Cuppa —

The Poetry of Tea

By Earlene Grey

Illustrated by Susan Laird

Copyright © 2009 Earlene Grey

POD Copyright © 2012 Earlene Grey

ISBN: 978-0-9843546-0-3 POD HB Version

All rights reserved.

Table of Contents

Foreword	7
Preface	9
To Those Who Ask	11
Chapter One – Musings on Life and Living	*1*
Question of the Ages	*1*
Tea in the Right Company — So Whom to Invite?	*3*
The Deceptive Invitation	*4*
The Sum of the Parts Is Greater Than the Whole	*4*
Dependency	*5*
No Need for Armour	*6*
Civility	*7*
To Be Healed	*8*
One Source (Variations From One Root)	*10*
The Opportunity of Chance	*11*
Of God	*12*
In Appreciation of the Unforeseen Answer	*12*
Don't Call the Teakettle Black	*13*
Sunday	*14*
The Assignment	*15*
The Hope of Spring	*16*
The Truth	*17*
The Opportunity of Warm and Quiet Evenings	*17*
The Autumn of Earth	*18*
Earth in the Fullness of Fall	*19*
In Defense of Rain	*20*
Tea in the Warmth of Winter	*21*
It Is the Gift That Counts	*22*
Christmas Tea	*23*
The Reading	*24*
Worth the Effort	*25*
The Opening of a Lifetime	*26*

Chapter Two — Musings on Friends and Family   27

Table of Your Life	27
Come Now My Dear	29
The Changing of the Guard	30
Wisdom Not Wasted	30
Age to Experience	31
Love of the Chintz Teacup	32
A Little Look Inside	33
For Now It's Time to Sleep	34
But Which First?	34
Ode to a Daughter	35
The "A" List	36
Warning From a Wiser Hostess	37
From One Who Knows	38
Someday	38
Friendship Tea	39
Comfort	40

Chapter Three — Musings on Love, Marriage, Men and More   41

True Love	41
Why Men to Tea?	43
Filled by the Cuppa	44
The Right Choice	45
Taking Tea and Kissing	46
The Tantalizing Taste of a Woman	47
Drawing the Qualities of a Woman	48
Tea and Delicacies	48
Full in Body	49
Do We Need to be Invigorated?	50
That Crucial Steeping Time	51
Iced Passion?	52
Not to the Point of Boiling	53
Go for the Pot	54
So Much to Discover	55
A Good Marriage	56
Invitation to Purpose	57
Marriages — Public or Private	58
Love Comes at Teatime	59

Let's Have a Cup of Tea	*59*
All We Need is a Cosy	*60*
Accompaniments	*61*
Resting in Anticipation	*62*

Chapter Four – Musings on Quietness   63

Tea With Me	*63*
Beyond Gold	*65*
In Quietness and In Confidence Shall Be Your Strength	*66*
Slow	*67*
Manna	*68*
A Favourite Teatime	*69*
Brave Artist	*70*
When You Want to Know	*71*
A Most Important Lesson in the Management of Life's Ups and Downs— What to Look for in the Right Teacup	*72*
A Decision Not to Know	*73*
The Surprise of the Quiet Conversion	*74*
The Truth About Secrets	*75*
Leaf Reading	*76*
Tea and Toil	*77*
Untitled	*78*

The world of tea is a wonderful place to be.

Foreword

If an all seeing Almighty sends you a poet named Earlene Grey who takes her inspirations from tea, be sure to read her. There are teachings in tea... and Earlene has learned any number of them. "A Good Marriage", for instance, according to her "...is not unlike tea. It takes a pleasing blend, warm hearts, secrets, steeping time (sometimes years) and a desire for that sweet taste of satisfied serenity."

No need to wonder how she and Earl Grey feel about each other. Sit down with a cup of his and this book of hers and see for yourself how they're simply made for one another's company.

James Norwood Pratt
San Francisco
10 December, 2005

Preface

Welcome to the world of Earlene Grey. Even though we are now firmly entrenched in the twenty-first century, turning the very first page of this book will take you back to the early twentieth century and the reign of England's King Edward VII.

Although the citizenry of Edwardian England was more relaxed and less formal than the society of Queen Victoria's day, the culture was still proper and full of optimism and abundance. It was a world that looked forward to a new century with eagerness and pride. It is the remembrance of this time that tea, poetry, and renewed enthusiasm for the simple pleasures of life have come together.

Musings With a Cuppa – The Poetry of Tea is a collection of original tea poetry that expresses the flavours and values of another era. The selections range from light-hearted innocence to humorous and saucy. But the intent is always to allow the reader to revel in the goodness of humanity that comes from combining a fine cuppa and the written word.

So calm your mind, have a cup of tea and savour poetry of a simpler time. Entering the world of Earlene Grey, if only for a moment, presents each individual with new opportunities to view life differently and gives new meaning to the word, teatime.

x

To Those Who Ask

I write because it is given.
I do not know why it comes to me.
I am only grateful for the opportunity.

Adding a good cup of tea
Is the extra treat I give to me.

Chapter One – Musings on Life and Living

Question of the Ages

Are we wiser
Because we have
Lived our youth?
Or younger
Because we have
Lived our wisdom?

Tea in the Right Company —
So Whom to Invite?

How imperfect are we
That we cannot find time for tea!

How we rush to be better,
To be sharper. To be more fine.
And yet we fail to fully live
In the wisdom of our time.

Perfection can be found most simply
By having the right company at tea.

Whether it is with those we love or,
With an angel stranger,
From that which is in front of us,
To that which eventually could be,
Our most perfect selves may be
Discovered by having the right company at tea.

The Deceptive Invitation

You pick the flowers.
I'll choose the tea.
You bake the cake.
I'll brew the tea.
You make the savouries.
I'll pour the tea.
No need for praises,
Just RSVP.

The Sum of the Parts Is Greater Than the Whole

Independence is not for us.
It doesn't work.
Our one simply doesn't add up to
The sum we need it to be.

Dependency

A wise man of God once said,
"We really do need each other."
It's true.
We do.

It is not men to men,
Or women to women,
Or any combination thereof.
It is simply, that all of us need all of us.

Whether it is a gentleman to his club,
Or a lady to her circle,
Or a loving couple at tea.
Each singularly fit into the fold.

It is not just in times of distress,
But also when there is no consequence.
It is a sweet fulfilling dependency that
Sings, "We really do need each other."

No Need for Armour

You and I are great souls.
And we come together for a time.
We meet over a cup of tea here on earth.

Shall we leave our shell and join with each other?
Shall we put down our shield and armour?
What will become of us if we do?
What horrible fate awaits us if we are defenseless?

Tea is a time for love and tenderness without fear.
It is a time for sharing and learning and growing.
Come now, leave the battle gear behind.
Brave with me and let's have tea.

Civility

Children hurt. Animals are vanquished.
Men and women weep.
War is rumored and hate is triumphant.
Oh, we foolish mortals!
If only reason and heart could come together.

Some would say that sitting and thinking and talking
With teacup in hand
And carefully being polite is a sham.

Yet how better to grow into civility?
For that's what we need.
The time to be polite,
To be honourable, to be sensible is now.

Why carry on with anger and pain and death?
Oh, you foolish mortals! Rise above.
Maybe, just maybe, the time for tea is now.

To Be Healed

History will tell of hard times,
Yours or mine,
When basic acts of
Existence demanded
Ultimate effort.
When pain was so common,
Awareness was lost.
And to merely continue on
Without knowing why
Was the only choice.

Knowing why may never come.
It might not matter.
But there are days of peace and
Safety that do come.
And joy that seeps in
Like water to a well.

When you are able to lift up a cup,
Drink some water
From the well.
A little each day,
As much as you can hold.
Then, as your thirst is quenched,
Share the water with another
Who is parched and weary.

And so it passes.
Weakness turns to strength.
Hurting flows to healing.
Judging moves to love.
We are whole again.

One Source (Variations From One Root)

Tea comes in many variations,
And so do we.
We naively think
There are many different kinds.
There are not.

Assam, Oolong, Earl Grey, English Breakfast,
Asian, Negroid, Hispanic,
Mongol, Caucasian.
Tea comes from one plant. One root.
And so do we.

We think, "Oh, this is a different tea."
It is not.
Just grown in a different place.
Just brought up differently.

Let us then not forego
The enjoyment of our own
Human variations,
Sometimes grown in a different place,
Brought up differently.
Variations from one root.

The Opportunity of Chance

Just when is it that we
Should hazard a risk?
Is it only when there will be
No pain at all? Or loss?

On the contrary.
We should take a risk
When our hearts pound and
Our breath quickens.
When fear is with us and
We know nothing else.

The lesson of chance is trust.
The reward of trust is bravery.
And the gratitude of bravery is wisdom.
You see it is not the outcome we obtain,
But it is the very act of doing
That gives to each his issue of success.

Of God

There is purpose in harmony.
There is divinity in choice.

It is the act of choosing that
Makes us victorious over humanity.

It is the right choice that
Makes us deserving of Divinity.

In Appreciation of the Unforeseen Answer

When looking for the answer
You only need to trust.
Knowing the question is not necessary.
Understanding that the answer will come, is.
And when the answer mysteriously appears,
It is only then that you can begin to
Gratefully appreciate the gracious and unexpected
Details of the master plan made for your behalf.

Don't Call the Teakettle Black

We were never totally good or
Perfect for the heart to see.
We are more likely better today
Than we were, and better yet to be.

We use one lens to visit those we love,
But a different glass when looking at ourselves.
All the time we are aware that each deserves
The Grace to be known for what he is,
And not for what he was.

Remember, then, not what was
Previously ill suited in others.
But choose your present over the past.
Celebrate the loves of your lives
As they grow with you, better yet to be at last.

Sunday

There are so many things to do.
Corners to clean, promises to keep.
Calls to make, problems to solve.
But not today. It's Sunday.

We're here with work to do
And lives to change.
With lessons to learn
And peace to make.

Things have to be done.
Parts to be fit to the whole.
Purposes to fulfill. Fruit to bear.
Our own charges to keep, without question.

But all in good time,
And at the right pace,
And all completed through God's own Grace.
But not today. It's Sunday.

So let us be happy.
Content, without care.
And let us make pots of cinnamon tea.
Especially today. It's Sunday.

The Assignment

It is not the fortunes we create,
Or the influence we have.
Not the merriment we share,
Or even the good we do.
Not the progeny we leave behind,
Or the discoveries we make.
It is not that we should aspire
To have a life well lived.
The goal is to have a life well used.

The Hope of Spring

Spring comes just when we need it to the most,
When there is no more waiting within us.
When one more dreary day cannot be tolerated,
Brown and gray are charmingly replaced by
Pink and yellow and green.

There is hope in the air of spring.
There is lightness and freedom, too.
So join me on my porch with a cuppa.
We will sit in freshness, smell new growth,
And smile in anticipation of
Even more that is yet to be.

The Truth

I am not fond of summer.
The air is hot and
The sun is bright.
It is impossible to sleep at night.

Were I so bold, and
The truth be told,
Summer is only right when
It is you and me and
Brandied tea at twilight.

The Opportunity of Warm and Quiet Evenings

Summer is you and me and
Tea at twilight,
Where we tell each other all
About nothing and come to know
The best of everything.

The Autumn of Earth

When the air is cool and warm
In the same day, and
You know that you
Will soon need to be inside,
But not yet,

You take a wrap and
Walk in the elegance of the
Brocaded landscape;
Or perhaps have tea
Under a tree to watch the
Animals ready for winter.

It is a sacred time of year.
This is favoured Autumn
That lets you bask
In Earth's brilliance.
And it is Scorpio's child
That bares her soul in
The beauty that you see.

Oh, Seasoned One,
Be wholly in her beauty.

Earth in the Fullness of Fall

When Earth, resplendent in colour,
Is stunning and deep with the
Richness for which we give thanks;
When the fruits of the soil
Reflect the fruits of the Spirit;
When our labour is done and
Rest is nigh;
Then is the time to relish
The brilliance of her fullness and
The time for a very special tea.

In Defense of Rain

Some aren't partial to it,
But I am.

Whether it is pouring hard or
Coming down softly,
Mercy drops from the heavens
Are cleansing and refreshing.

It is not hot or humid,
Nor does it dry or burn.
It is perfect for warm tea, buttered scones,
And looking out in calm reflection.

Tea in the Warmth of Winter

Come with me into my fantasy of winter
Where snow falls softly and all is silent.
Where each and every creature has a
Warm place without fear of cold or death.

Come with me into my fantasy where
We will have tea in my parlour and
Savour each quiet moment of peace
And revel in our own little world of Grace.

It Is the Gift That Counts

High Tea on Christmas Day
With friends and family
Close and warm and safe.
With sugar cakes and savouries
And spiced tea from the chest.

True, it is the celebration of
God's gift to all of us,
But more important still,
It is what we will bestow
On all of those who are
But one small
Grace away from us.

Christmas Tea

Christmas is Christ time.
God is with us.
Emmanuel.

That the Spirit is here
To guide and to help
Is clear to me and to you.

Since this is so, let us not be troubled.
Nor be anxious, nor be fretful.
Ever.

Let go of worry. Have Christmas Tea.
Remember that God is with us.
Gloria.
Gloria.
Halleluiah.
And Halleluiah again.

The Reading

A star called Moon
Came and showed me light.
I couldn't see and didn't know
What was around and above and below.

Moon talked of angels and dragons,
Of roses, and butterflies, and of Michael.
I wasn't aware of the care
That was being taken for my sake.

But she knew.
And Moon shared the secrets.
For tealeaves can heal and heal again.
Whether lovingly steeped or wisely read,
They can bring you rest and care
While you are gracefully being led.

Worth the Effort

It is not the years we live,
With the tears that fall.

It is the smiles we share,
Along the miles we travel.

It is the cakes we serve
And the tea we pour.

It is these things and more,
The sustenance of life and love,
That makes who we are,
Celebrated above and revered below.

The Opening of a Lifetime

When you open one door,
You can live a thousand lifetimes.
Just one door to walk through
On the way to that which is not known.
The turn of the knob and the slight push
On the panel can expand a life
To more than the imagination
Can see.
Open the door.

Chapter Two —
Musings on Friends and Family

Table of Your Life

At the table of your life
Make room for tea,
And make room for me,
And make room for friends and family
And we will make room for thee.

Come Now My Dear

Come now my Dear,
And we shall have
A cup of tea and a glass
Of reverie.

We shall sit and sip
And gossip and laugh
And sigh and sip again.

For tea brings forth secrets and
Sensibilities at the same time.
So when we drink, we will know
With calm assurety just where
We find ourselves to be.

The Changing of the Guard

Friends can change in person and in place.
Many of mine have come and gone.
But it doesn't matter who comes when
And why and for how long,
Because a friend is good for whatever can be wrong.

Wisdom Not Wasted

Birthdays come and go
And sadly so do friends.
But what we have left
Is what we know.

So take what you know,
Send it with prayers and peace
To friends and foe alike.
Then take tea with cream and sugar
And let all the rest go.

Age to Experience

From age to experience,
From wisdom to grace,
To flow from one to another,
Should certainly be done at
One's own pace.

From age to experience,
From wisdom to grace,
To flow from one to another,
Just may be a true
And simple release.

From age to experience,
From wisdom to grace,
To flow from one to another,
Is that which brings to
The soul its sweet completeness.

Love of the Chintz Teacup

Where spirits are lifted
And minds are renewed.
Where dreams are born
And our souls find rest.

Not simply a place, but more.
Not only one heart, but many.
Where friends and strangers gather to meet
And to know only the best.

It is the beautiful Mum
Who ensures our dreams and memories.
It is she who draws up
Recipes for visions of plenty.

It is Mum who creates the Chintz legacy,
Beauty from patterns.
Memories from sincerity.
It is she who will ever make
The Chintz the perfect spot for tea.

A Little Look Inside

Could there be a little old lady
In each one of us?
Even you men of hardened steel?
Yes, little old ladies.
You know the kind,
Sweet and sage and oh, so serene.

The question is asked because
All is not as it seems.
Little old ladies can be
Just plain naughty,
Deliciously surprising and
Insightfully insane.

So I urge you, curious soul,
Invite a little old lady to tea
And see, not with a big surprise,
Just how little,
How old,
And how like a lady
You can be.

For Now It's Time to Sleep

Trundle off to bed with me
And we will have sweet dreams of
Silvery moons and cats and spoons,
Then waken the dawn with
Tea and scones and apple jam.

But Which First?

Shall we have a nap or take tea?
For nap time and tea time
Go hand in hand.

And if the tea is sweet
And the sleep is warm,
Then the secrets of
Tea leaves and dreamscapes
We will joyfully understand.

Ode to a Daughter

My daughter you are just perfect.
You are more than everything
You need to be.

You are a lovely taste of this and that
Blended flawlessly to be a
Soothing cup of tea.

You are the essence of Assam
And the majesty of Darjeeling.
You are Sweet Asia served like Jasmine
In a perfect cup of tea.

The "A" List

Kittens are your very best guests for tea.
They won't require Albert's china.
When serving milk and savouries,
A chipped saucer will do just fine.

They will sit quietly and enjoy
Your company
And never say,
"So tell me, Dear,
What is it exactly that you do?"

Kittens are cute,
Generally quiet and mostly free.
Could there ever be
A better invitee for tea?

Warning From a Wiser Hostess

The tarts were out.
Savouries set.
Cream for fruit well chilled.
Guests were chatting and the
Hostess glowing.
Sencha with grandeur was served.

Then just at the moment when
All were gazing at the garden,
Uninvited to be sure,
Miss Kitty came to tea.

Up on the table she jumped,
Sending titters of shocks in waves.
Searching for a treat,
She took a taste of this and that,
Quite nearly upsetting the pot!

Then faster than the hand could move,
Off jumped Kitty racing to reach
The far end corner of the room.
And there she sat, smugly licking,
Savouring the treats she stole from me.

Oh, what calamity and chaos
No doubt there will be—
When Miss Kitty comes to tea!

From One Who Knows

One cat is sweet.
Two kitties are cute.
Three cats are plenty.
Four are too many.

Someday

Soon I will be free.
Without tightness or propriety.
Sans care and sensibility.

And when I am free,
I will sit in the sun
And drink tea
With cuties and kitties,

Never minding what
Others might see,
Ever laughing at what
They might say.

Friendship Tea

Either for a lifetime or
Just a little while,
Some people need many friends.
Others need just one or two
Honest souls to walk with them
Along the way.
Whichever I am to you,
Or you are to me,
Let us take tea and
Enjoy our marvelous company.

Comfort

Rest with me, my Love.
Calm down your mind.
  Release your pain.

Rest with me, my Love.
Let go of your hurry.
  Undo your cares.

Rest with me, my Dear
Put down your fears,
  Begin to heal.
Let me give you a heart of chamomile.

Chapter Three —

Musings on Love, Marriage, Men and More

True Love

Said Pot to his darling, Cup,
"It's tea with you and me, Dear,
It's tea with you and me.
For all I know and all I see,
There is nothing better than
Tea with you and me."

Why Men to Tea?

So why should we compare men to tea?
Both are wonderful to me.

Considering each is to amuse,
Providing insight if ever we had to choose.

Men take a great deal of care.
Tea does not; it is easy to prepare.

Tea stays warms only for a song.
A man can keep you cosy all night long.

There are differences indeed, but
Both can be vital to the ladies' world.
Whether each is bitter or is sweet,
Both can make a lady's life complete.

Filled by the Cuppa

There are many reasons why we take tea.
But I must say that
Toasting one's object of affection
Must certainly be the most delighting.

A wink, a nod, a smile,
All are appropriate and admirable
Dalliances at tea.

So lift up your cuppa.
Tilt it slightly toward your target.
Look your love square in the eye,
Raise your brow slightly and
Smile a secret invitation.

Then wait for the knowing
And glowing response
That only you will see.
Then both you and your love will say,
"Oh, what fulfillment comes from tea!"

The Right Choice

It may take two or three tea tastings
To find the type that is right for you.
And so it is with men.
Do not assume that the first one
You sample is your premium choice.

Dear Ladies, try a few out and then
Make your selection carefully.
Because men, like tea, offer
Many flavours, but there will always
Be just one favourite that you will
Want to enjoy every morning.

It is only a matter of practicality, my Dear.

Taking Tea and Kissing

The pastimes of kissing and that of drinking
A satisfyingly smooth cup of tea
Are very similar,
Delightful.

We may enjoy the warmth and the taste
And the pleasure far too long.
But when we do,
Contentment is within our reach.

It stands to reason therefore,
That we must kiss and take tea daily.
But, please my Dear,
Do so only with an admirer
That truly enjoys the amusement
Just as enthusiastically as we.

The Tantalizing Taste of a Woman

With tea what you get for taste
Is what you choose to brew.
If you select premium whole leaves,
Not ground up bits of dust, then you
Will get a richer flavour that
Will tempt you time and time again.

The qualities of a good woman
Are much the same.
It's the whole woman you
Should consider, not specks of
This and that which can be
Whisked away like spilled leaves on
The counterboard.

Choosing a good woman
May take many tastings and much time.
But making the right
Choice will be oh, so rewarding–
When you enjoy cup, after cup,
After cup, after cup.

Drawing the Qualities of a Woman

If you want to get the
Best from a woman,
Treat her as you would
Treat fine tea.
House her well.
Appreciate her delicate properties.
Put her to your lips often and
Savour her enhancing qualities.

Tea and Delicacies

There are so many flavours one can enjoy.
Not all are served on a plate.
Come and let me taste.
Let me enjoy the delicacies you have to offer.

Then I will delight and grow fat from the feast.
And I will be round and plump and pleased,
And full from the flavour of your love.

Full in Body

A first rate cup of tea
Is like a wonderful man.
Full in body.
Rich in flavour.
Clear of heart.

Some men have the stirrings
Of youthful excitement,
But can be weak and thin,
Without the strength of wisdom.

I prefer my men
Smooth and full,
With no guessings of
Hidden flavours or
Teasings of odd blends.

It's true.
A hearty self-drinking tea and
A good man can bring a great deal of
Satisfaction, even to the experienced taster.

So take my advice, Ladies, and look for
The full in body and clear of heart.
Then I'm sure you, too, will enjoy
The rich in flavour.

Do We Need to be Invigorated?

Some ladies like their
Tea brisk and bracing.
But what does tea
Brace them for?

Would that be true of their men too?
I think men, like tea,
Should be refreshing
Only by their calming qualities.

Look then for the temperament of chamomile,
Not the nature of caffeine.
Enjoy what men and tea
Have to offer, but take in only
What is soothing and serene.

That Crucial Steeping Time

Men are like tea leaves.
Getting in hot water for just
A little while produces
An interesting and tantalizing flavour.

Too long in hot water
Creates a bitter taste,
And can make for a
Very unpleasant experience.

So Ladies, whether brewing tea leaves or men,
Don't worry about them being in hot water.
Let them steep for just the
Right amount of time and you, too,
Will savour the flavour of
Your favourite cup of tea.

Iced Passion?

Don't give me any of that iced tea,
With chunks of coldness
Floating in it like death
Waiting for the Titanic.

I want my tea hot.
Hot tea has soul.
Like passionate lovers
In a downy bed.

Yes, let's have tea
And warm our senses.
Let's have tea
And drink in the steaming passion.

Not to the Point of Boiling

One reason that we like tea is
Because it is hot.

The same might be said of men too,
But it is not
Because we ladies keep them
At a rolling boil.

It is, conversely,
Because we keep
Them calm and cool.

Go for the Pot

Some people invite one to have a cuppa.
Others offer invitations of more.

Whether the invitation is one of
Tea, laughter, love or more,
I prefer to have a pot.
And then another.

So when you are offering tea,
Do not be miserly.
Make a pot. Drink it down.
Make another and then
Really get down to
The business of what
You had in store.

So Much to Discover

Men are glorious Creatures,
Their features are so
Interesting to sort out,
We wonder what they are really all about.

It is not always easy to understand
What a man can comprehend,
But it is always a pleasure to discover
Their marvelous talents in the end.

A Good Marriage

A good cup of tea just doesn't happen.
It takes a warm pot, good water,
The right amount of time,
And a few additional secrets
Known only to those who are not satisfied
With the tepid tasteless.

Marriage is not unlike tea.
It takes a pleasing blend,
Warm hearts, secrets,
Steeping time (sometimes years) and
A desire for that sweet taste of satisfied serenity.

Ah, to sit and savour a great cup of tea is truly
A bit of heaven on earth.
The right ingredients, the right time.
And so it is with a sweet marriage.
The right ingredients, the right time.
A bit of heaven here on earth.

Invitation to Purpose

We are great souls.
And we were made for a
Glorious purpose.
The work is done and
The foundation is laid.
I am becoming the
Woman I was meant to be.
You are emerging too.
Shall we go together and rise
To what we were surely born to be?

Marriages — Public or Private

Some marriages come with
Big pronouncements and productions,
Shouting the news for all to hear.

Other marriages come modestly.
So modestly that even the bride and groom
May not be aware when it appears.
Marriages can leave in the very same way.
Quietly or with much ado.

Whether you are letting your union go
Or sending it away,
When you turn to lean on your marriage,
And it is no more,
The void that is left may surprise
And leave you empty and forlorn.

So sit with your wedded Soul.
Pour each other a cup of tea.
Inquire as to whether your Love
Might prefer lemon or sugar—
Then fill each other up.

And not to worry whether
Your marriage is public or private, loud or quiet
Only that you and your Love are each other's
Personal cup of tea.

Love Comes at Teatime

"Sit with me," my husband says,
"And have a cup of tea."

I devour four cups
To his one,
His talking being slower
Than my drinking.

How sweet to listen
And to savour
The time and the flavour and the tea.
For love truly does come at Teatime.

Let's Have a Cup of Tea

Come and teach me who you are.
I long to love.
I long to feel joy.
Will you be my peace?
Will you be my strength?
Come have tea with me.
Let us drink in each other's soul
And see what answers there may be.

All We Need is a Cosy

I am the leaves.
You are the pot.
I give you joy
And you steep my
Passion, first to hold
And then to gently pour out.

I unfurl and twirl and
Swirl about, while you
Subtly contain me
And together we blend,
Steep our lives
And serve our teatime love.

Accompaniments

Men and women belong together,
Like presented cream and sugar, side by side.
Complementing, finishing and satisfying
They can sweeten the bitter,
And strengthen the weak.

So dear Reader, in living life as in serving tea,
It is the blend of accompaniments
We carefully add to the cup
That makes the taste complete.

Resting in Anticipation

I have been told that there
Will be good times.
That the time for struggle has passed.
And the time to rest in now.
All will be taken care of.
Good things will come.

So, if you please, my Dear,
Have tea with me and
Let us enjoy with confidence
And without cruel reserve,
The anticipating of our peace.

Chapter Four – Musings on Quietness

Tea With Me

Tea with one's self is truly fine.
I do it all the time.

There is so much to learn,
And so little to alarm,
That discussing my deepest secrets
Is effort free when it's
Just between me and me.

Beyond Gold

To sit quietly
And let everything
And everyone go by
Is truly a treasure
Not everyone can enjoy.

Sitting so with tea in hand,
Many thoughts can crowd the mind.
But it's sitting so with tea in hand,
To see what fills the heart—
That's the truest treasure one can have.

In Quietness and In Confidence Shall Be Your Strength

Quietness comes and goes.
It cannot be forced.
It has to be coaxed.

Even though all around
There might be stillness,
One's mind can be full of noise.

So it is up to each one alone
To call forth the Quietness,
Let it steep in our mind,
And gently pour it into our Soul.
Then, when we have our Quietness,
It is promised that we will Know.

Slow

For heaven's sake, Dear,
Sip, sip.

One gulps coffee, swills beer,
And swigs whiskey.
But one sips tea.
We slow down and sip tea.

Manna

Tea and toast,
Tea and toast.
Of all the great suppers,
It's the one I love the most.

A Favourite Teatime

According to Janet, a good time
To have tea is right after the post.
Sitting in Solitude nonchalantly perusing
Letters and catalogues is a delight.
To others the whole pastime may sound boring,
Dull or desperate, but surprisingly enough,
It is wonderfully satisfying.

As always, presentation counts.
Even when in the company of one's self,
Making the right impression is crucial.
One must have china and crystal,
Not porcelain and pottery.
It is quietness, order, beauty and taste
Which brings moments of appreciated peace.

It is not the multitude's idea of a special tea.
Some do not know, nor
Could they possibly conceive of
How joyful it is to sit and revel
In the small masterpieces
Of the daily mail, Solitude and tea.

Brave Artist

How brave the artist.
The soul who holds the great
Secrets of Humanity in
His heart, but is often left
Alone to bare the burden.

How brave is he who
Shares that which is within.
How brave the man who
Claims his purpose and
Carries on despite the pain.

How brave the artist,
The keeper of our Souls.

When You Want to Know

It is not easy to understand
The quiet person.
Their secrets are not out in front
For all to see and hear.

To learn what a quiet person knows,
You have to ask and ask again.
Then take them to tea,
And ask again persistently.

But once they tell, it all makes sense.
"Oh!", you say, "I was so dense,
Mrs. Quiet is such a marvel.
She knows so much. And she sees so far."

To be part of society, quiet people
Learn to be loud, to be noisy.
It is not fun, nor is it easy. For them
Being quiet is being genuine, exquisitely.

So when you want to know—
Trust a quiet person.
Then just ask. Ask again,
And then be sure to listen.

A Most Important Lesson in the Management of Life's Ups and Downs— What to Look for in the Right Teacup

It is crucial to have
Just the right teacup
When celebrating life's blessings or
When contemplating its challenges.

There are many options to choose from.
Minimally, the cup must be
Deep enough to maintain warmth and
The handle round enough for
A good strong hold.

As for its composition,
Bone china, of course.
And finally, you must carefully select the
Pattern to match your current disposition.

This basic ability will carry you,
Not only when life is more than pleasant
And friends are fond and numerous,
But through disharmonious times and with
A wide variety of vexing and disagreeable people
Who, shall we say, aren't exactly your cup of tea.

A Decision Not to Know

Sometimes I am defined by what I do,
Trying to make what I do, into who I am.
Yet spinning about so from one to another me
Weakens the mind and binds the soul.

Sometimes who one is has to be said
And then it must be owned.
But who is to say what and why and when?

Is it for me to say and be and then to do?
Or shall I just do and then I will be?
I truly haven't a clue.

Well then, what?
"Have tea!" I say to those who query,
"And leave me quietly and respectfully be!"

Amen.

The Surprise of the Quiet Conversion

Things come softly to you and me.
Most of the time we don't
Even realize the presence of
The Source, the pathway or the passage.
We just know that our lives are different.
Sometimes we even realise
Our lives are better.

The Truth About Secrets

All of us have secrets.
There are those of us with
Stories that do not need to be told.
Some of us hide what must be healed.
And others alone are privy to his own special promise.

If what you conceal is frightening because of pain, let it out.
If your secret is one of promise, keep it close.
Regardless of what you do, remember,
You are not alone in your mysteries.
All of us have secrets—some—the same as yours.

Leaf Reading

What is it that we are supposed to do?
Work or play or live life as
Best we can day by day.
Surely the answer is none of these.

We all have talents endowed to us
By the great I Am.
They are ours to keep or
To invest as best we can.

Would it not be most satisfying
To all concerned if our work and play
Were to give away
The talents that we renew?
What profits we would see!

So then let it be.
That which is given to us,
Shall be given away.
Justifiably, if that is our work,
And that is our nature,
Then with sensibility,
It is our earthly reason to be.

Tea and Toil

Work is overrated.
It is a necessity, an admonition,
Fulfilling and enlightening,
A gift for humankind,
But still overrated.

So please, Dear Industrious One,
In the midst of your working,
In the midst of your doing,
Take time for tea and
Find the reason for your being.

Untitled

As I pass through this world
And do my work
And drink my tea,
I wonder if there will ever be
A little left of me.

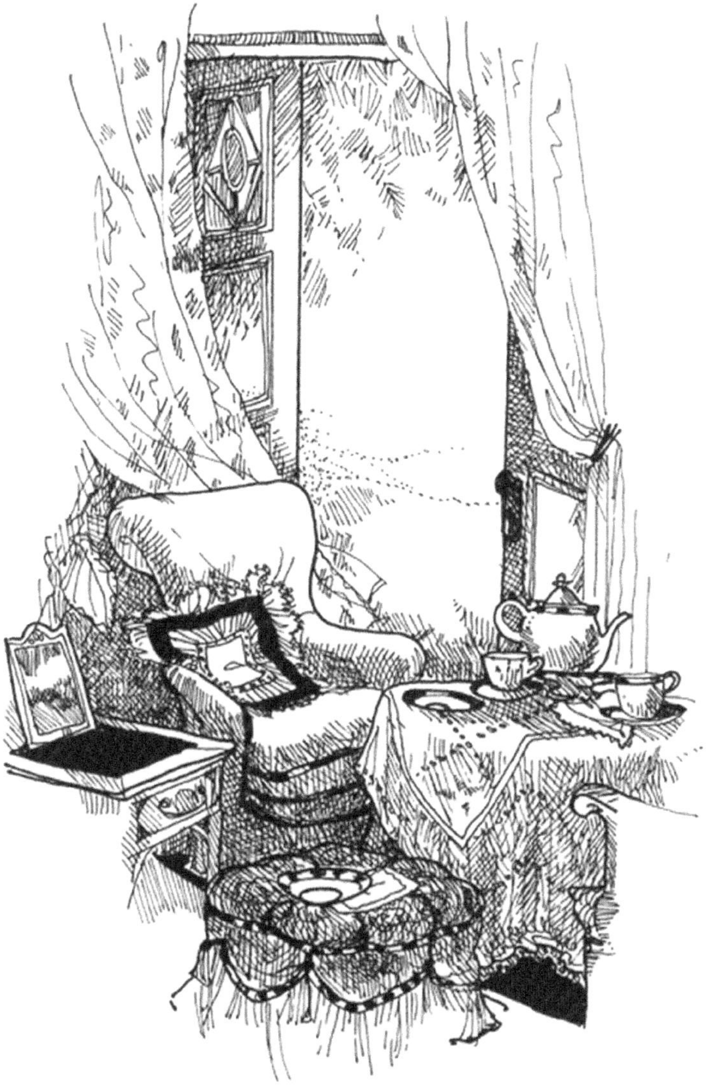

You may never know what extraordinary good you do by serving someone a cup of tea ~ so do it often.

Earlene Grey

CPSIA information can be obtained at www.ICGtesting.com
Printed in the USA
LVOW01*1042030914

402168LV00001B/1/P